The Bus Ride

Written by Anne Mclean   Illustrated by Leslie Wolf

ScottForesman

A Division of HarperCollinsPublishers

A girl got on the bus.

Then the bus went fast.

A boy got on the bus.

Then the bus went fast.

A fox got on the bus.

Then the bus went fast.

A hippopotamus got on the bus.

Then the bus went fast.

A goat got on the bus.

Then the bus went fast.

A rhinoceros got on the bus.

Then the bus went fast.

A fish got on the bus.

Then the bus went fast.

A horse got on the bus.

Then the bus went fast.

A rabbit got on the bus.

Then the bus went fast.

A bee got on the bus.

Then!

 The rabbit got off the bus.

 The horse got off the bus.

 The fish got off the bus.

 The rhinoceros got off the bus.

 The goat got off the bus.

 The hippopotamus got off the bus.

 The fox got off the bus.

 The boy got off the bus.

 The girl got off the bus.

Then they all ran fast!